Original title:
Gravity-Defying Rhymes

Copyright © 2025 Creative Arts Management OÜ
All rights reserved.

Author: Jude Lancaster
ISBN HARDBACK: 978-1-80567-816-8
ISBN PAPERBACK: 978-1-80567-937-0

Floating Verses in a Starlit Sky

In a sky where socks take flight,
And cows leap high, without a fright.
The moon is laughing, full of glee,
As stars play hopscotch, wild and free.

Words drift up like cotton candy,
Each rhyme's a bouncy bit too dandy.
Jokes balloon, they float and sway,
In this wacky, weightless play.

The Weightless Waltz of Words

Words are dancing, what a sight,
Twisting, turning, in pure delight.
They glide on breezes, light as air,
Doing the cha-cha without a care.

Sentences leap, they spin and twirl,
Making the grammar do a whirl.
With laughter, they slide across the floor,
Cracking jokes, then asking for more.

Ascending with the Moon's Embrace

Up we go, in moonlit bliss,
Each line a hug, each pause a kiss.
We bounce on beams, like it's a game,
And giggle loud, calling names in fame.

Thoughts float up like bubbles bright,
Bursting softly with sheer delight.
In this ascent, humor ignites,
As words sprout wings and reach new heights.

Poems that Defy the Ground

Bouncing lines that skip and hop,
They never land, they love to plop.
Doodles dance on clouds of fluff,
In this world, never enough!

Puns take flight, on birdie's wings,
They chirp and giggle, oh the sings!
So join the fun, just lift your pen,
Let laughter rise, again and again.

Verses on the Breeze

A bird once wore a tiny hat,
He thought it made him look quite fat.
He tried to dance upon a stream,
But ended up in a loud scream.

A cloud transformed into a chair,
For squirrels having picnic flair.
They sipped on nectar, ate some pie,
Then flew away, oh my! Oh my!

Navigating the Ether

The fish decided to fly high,
With wings made of a pizza pie.
He soared above a surfing cat,
Who caught a wave, how 'bout that!

A frog played chess with a kite,
In a game that lasted all night.
With every move, the wind would tease,
As they avoided bumblebees!

Elevated Echoes

An ant once climbed a balloon,
He thought he'd reach the stars quite soon.
But halfway up, he lost his way,
And ended up in a birthday fray.

A donut tried to spin and glide,
But rolled away, oh what a ride!
It bounced on clouds and sang a tune,
Disappearing with the afternoon.

A Flight of Fancy

A turtle dreamed of flying fast,
While lounging in the sun, he laughed.
With a jetpack made of bread and cheese,
He zoomed through trees with frantic ease.

A rabbit danced on stilts of air,
While juggling carrots without a care.
His friends all cheered, they couldn't wait,
For his next big airborne plate!

Updrafts of Imagination

A kite once told a windy tale,
Of how it danced without a sail.
With every gust, it touched the sky,
And giggled at the passersby.

A bird on stilts, a daring feat,
Waltzing through the air on feet.
It claimed to be a king, so grand,
In a realm of fluff, where dreams expand.

Lofty Pronouncements

The clouds grew tired of their own fluff,
And decided they had seen enough.
With a chuckle, they shed a tear,
To rain a sprinkle of silly cheer.

A squirrel bought a rocket pack,
Zooming high, but oh, what a crack!
He flew past moon and stars so bright,
Then realized he forgot the flight.

The Height of Artistry

An artist painted with a twist,
A canvas where the colors kissed.
The brush took flight, a soaring spree,
Above the easel, wild and free.

A cat in a top hat, quite absurd,
Recited verses, hardly heard.
His whiskers twitched with every rhyme,
As he danced upon the edge of time.

Dreams on the Updraft

A dreamer bounced on marshmallow clouds,
Reciting jokes to playful crowds.
With every punchline, up they flew,
In laughter's lift, their spirits grew.

A penguin in a tutu waltzed,
Ignoring all the snow that balled.
He slid and twirled, a comical sight,
In a frosty soirée, just so bright.

Verses on the Edge of Atmosphere

Up above the world so high,
Where squirrels wear their ties and fly.
Penguins in tuxes, oh what a sight,
Dancing in clouds on a starry night.

Balloons turn into zeppelins brave,
And all the cats just need a rave.
Kites are plotting a wild escape,
While turtles glide in a dreamy drape.

Unshackled From the Soil

Ants in space with their tiny dreams,
Swing on the stars, plotting their schemes.
Bees buzzing tunes to tickle the moons,
Playing hopscotch with the luminous tunes.

Marshmallows float, not a worry or care,
Pillows in parades, dance in mid-air.
Lollipops swirl in a candy parade,
While chia pets play charades in the shade.

Lyrical Elevation

Balloons burst into a symphony grand,
With tasty treats and lemonade stand.
Frogs in tuxedos leap through the mist,
High-fiving the ducks, can you resist?

Clouds play hopscotch, clouds play tag,
The sun throws darts, can you brag?
Lemonade rivers flowing with cheer,
Fill up your glasses and bring good cheer.

Songs of Airborne Inspiration

Chickens in capes, soaring so high,
Flip-flopping in style, oh my, oh my!
Giggles of breezes whisper and sway,
As dandelions join the ballet.

Shoelaces dancing, they twirl and spin,
Even the socks want to join in!
With laughter that echoes, we float away,
In a world where whimsy likes to play.

Lightfooted Musings

On my toes, I dance with glee,
Floating like a bumblebee.
I trip and tumble, then I bounce,
Defying balance, like a flounce.

A jellybean in frosty air,
I laugh at gravity's despair.
A pirouette, I take a leap,
In a world where heights are cheap.

Skyward Bound

With a hop, I leave the ground,
Turning upside down and round.
I wonder if the moon plays cards,
While I juggle invisible guards.

Each twist and turn brings giggles bright,
As I soar toward the rainbow's light.
A trampoline of silly dreams,
Where even clouds burst at the seams.

Aerial Reflections

Like a kite on a breezy day,
I flip and flop in a playful way.
Mirrors up high all show me grins,
While I swirl in a dance of spins.

I see my friends on a cotton cloud,
We leap and sway, our laughter loud.
What fun to float and glide and tease,
In a frolicsome world of air and ease.

Heights of Inspiration

In the air, ideas take flight,
A wacky whimsy, pure delight.
I climb on dreams, I tumble down,
A king of fun in my silly crown.

Bouncing high, I catch a star,
Who knew the sky was so bizarre?
I giggle as I drift above,
In the heights of pure, unfiltered love.

Nimbus Narratives

In a world where balloons float with glee,
The cats wear jetpacks, oh can't you see!
A snail on a skateboard speeds by with flair,
While fish ride unicycles up in the air.

Worms have begun to form a band,
Playing tunes on guitars, isn't it grand?
The daisies don hats, oh what a sight!
They dance with the breeze, lost in delight.

A parrot in shades struts down the lane,
Cracking jokes about the local train.
The squirrels are hosting a picnic so fine,
With acorn cake and grape soda divine.

In this land filled with whimsy and cheer,
Laughter erupts from all that is near.
So come join the fun in this silly spree,
Where laughter and joy fly wild and free!

Aerial Aria

Penguins in parachutes, gliding with grace,
Noses to the sky in this aerial race.
Balloons filled with giggles drift up and away,
While turtles on hang gliders shout, 'What a day!'

A dog in a cape races clouds in the blue,
Chasing after rainbows, oh what a view!
The owls have formed a book club on high,
Discussing the latest in clouds passing by.

Bouncing on trampolines, frogs leap with style,
Dancing on air, they go wild for a while.
There's a spider who weaves a net made of cheer,
Catching the giggles that drift ever near.

The sun wears sunglasses; it's hot in the sky,
While shoes play tag, oh my, oh my!
In this whimsical land where nonsense runs free,
Every twist and turn adds to the spree!

Ether's Embrace

In the sky, a cow took flight,
With a parachute made of light.
She giggled as she soared so high,
Sipping clouds and pie from the sky.

A cat in socks danced on the breeze,
Wiggling its tail with absolute ease.
It caught a bird, or so it claimed,
But both just laughed, and nothing's maimed.

A Poetic Flight

A rabbit with a jetpack hat,
Zoomed past a sleepy, dreaming cat.
He laughed and spun in loops of glee,
While saying, "Catch me if you please!"

An elephant wore roller skates,
Twirling around like he had plates.
He slipped and slid across the grass,
A funny sight—a real first class!

Sunlit Echoes on the Breeze

A squirrel with shades flew down a hill,
Chasing after acorns with great thrill.
He shouted to the sun, "Hold tight!"
As he twirled in a comic flight.

Bees started buzzing like a tune,
Bouncing high into the afternoon.
They danced on flowers, laughing loud,
Feeling bright and ever proud.

The Art of Leaping into Air

A frog on a trampoline took the leap,
Flying so high, he'd barely peep.
With cartwheels and flips, he stole the show,
As onlookers gasped, "Where did he go?"

A penguin in a top hat flew,
Waddling and flapping, true and true.
He landed smooth on a passing boat,
Sipping tea while wearing a coat.

Skyward Bound: A Poetic Lilt

A kite flew into the neighbor's yard,
As two kids chased it, running hard.
The dog thought it was a brand new friend,
But the kids just laughed as they raced to mend.

With a dozen balloons, a boy took flight,
His mom yelled, "Careful!" with all her might.
He floated past trees, a ballooning joke,
Waving down at the laughing folk.

Levitating Letters of Light

A pencil dances, scribbles in the air,
Words do the cha-cha, without a care.
Paper's a trampoline, bouncing so high,
Sentences giggle, they soar and fly.

Ink blobs are jumping, a silly parade,
Wiggling and tumbling as if they are played.
Each stroke a circus act, wild and bright,
In this playful realm, there's no end in sight.

The Untamed Flight of Ink

A inkpot's glee, spilling tales at will,
Letters on wings, a quirky thrill.
Twirling and swirling, they sway like a dance,
Making us chuckle, at every chance.

With every droplet, a giggle takes flight,
Voices in loops, a comical sight.
Sentences waltz, all dressed in cheer,
Who knew words had such a sense of sphere?

Beyond the Blue: Untethered Words

Up in the clouds, the nouns cavort,
Adjectives bounce—they're quite the sport.
Verbs stretch their legs, in a playful race,
While conjunctions giggle, keeping up the pace.

Exclamations leap, oh, what a hoot!
Dancing through sentences, oh, how they scoot!
In this topsy-turvy, whimsical flight,
Words play tag till the end of the night.

Ascension Above the Tethered Heart

Hearts don't sink, they twirl and twine,
Love letters soar, as if on a vine.
They float like feathers, so soft and spry,
Bouncing on breezes, they laugh and sigh.

In the sky of joy, every poem sings,
Tickling the clouds, on fluttering wings.
Each phrase is a balloon, bright and free,
Taking our worries, oh, wait and see!

Poem Above the Earth

Up in the sky, I feel so light,
Dancing with clouds, what a sight!
Birds join in, they flap and sing,
While I float on a carrot wing.

Down below, the world looks small,
People waving like a tiny doll.
I'm the king of the cartwheeling air,
In my bubble, without a care.

When I trip, I just bounce around,
Like a jelly bean that's not quite found.
What a thrill, this floating spree,
With laughter ringing, wild and free.

Uplifted Lines

In the whirlwind, I lose my shoe,
Chasing dreams, what can I do?
Tongue-tied in the fun we create,
All my worries levitate.

With a hop, skip, and a giggle, so bright,
I flip through space like a really fast kite.
Tickling the stars, it's quite a game,
With every tumble, I forget my name.

Here in the air, all floats are grand,
Conversations drift, just like sand.
In this realm where silliness reigns,
Life's a circus, with joy that remains.

Light as a Feather

On a pogo stick, I bounce so high,
Like a popcorn kernel, ready to fly.
With a wink and a twist, I soar with pride,
Each giggle a springboard to the wide side.

Fluffy clouds hear my jokes so true,
While moonbeams laugh, they join the crew.
With each leap, I'm flying too,
Like a sock that's lost the other shoe.

Every tumble is a happy surprise,
As I dance with leaves, beneath laughing skies.
Joining the breeze, take off where I please,
Life is a comedy, with moments that tease.

Language on a Breeze

Words take flight on a summer's air,
Whispers floating everywhere.
A joke, a pun, they twist and turn,
Through the laughter, my heart will yearn.

Riding the currents, we giggle and flip,
On a merry-go-round, we loosely grip.
Each chuckle rises, a balloon so bright,
In this dance of delight, we take our flight.

Floating high, we lose our mind,
In this riddle of joy, we unconfined.
As the sunshine rolls, we spin and twirl,
A caper of words sends us all in a whirl.

Surreal Skies

In a world where cows can fly,
Pigs wear capes and wave goodbye.
Chickens dance with joyful glee,
Bouncing high like a bee on spree.

Umbrellas float on cotton candy,
While frogs sing tunes quite dandy.
A sun that laughs and winks so bright,
Makes clouds giggle with pure delight.

A fish swims by in a top hat,
Telling jokes, how lovely is that?
Mountains roll like soft, warm bread,
And clouds are pillows for sleepy heads.

Starlit Flutter

Fireflies waltz in the evening glow,
While stars parade with a dazzling show.
The moon jests, "I'm a floating pie,"
As giggling comets zoom on by.

Wishes ride on a kite's long tail,
Tickled by the whimsical gale.
Ducks in tuxedos take to the sky,
Chasing the breeze, oh my, oh my!

The night is alive with snickers and cheer,
As shadows play tag, they disappear.
Whimsical worlds held in laughter tight,
Where dreams can fly into the night.

Gravity's Gentle Rebellion

Ants in boots on a trampoline,
Jumping high, a silly scene.
The grass shouts, "Come play with me!"
As frogs breakdance with wild glee.

A cat in shades, lounging on air,
Sipping tea without a care.
Napping clouds with a snooze so loud,
Cheering on the levitating crowd.

The flowers flip in cartwheeled bliss,
Nature's acrobats, none to miss.
With laughter light in a world so grand,
Where silliness reigns at a joyful stand.

Rise of the Poetic Spirits

With giggles rising like warm balloons,
The sun plants jokes on afternoons.
A chorus of quirks in a playful line,
Spirits twirl to a melody divine.

Balloons with faces float all around,
They crack jokes, making silly sounds.
Twirling daisies in a dance of cheer,
Jumping over moonbeams, oh so near.

In the garden where laughter grows,
Witty wonders burst and glow.
Dancing leaves tell tales anew,
As poetic spirits take their view.

Horizons Unhinged

In space, my socks just float away,
They dance around, they love to play.
The moon says, "Hey, where's your shoe?"
I laugh and say, "It's off to view!"

My coffee cup is now a kite,
It sways and dips, what a delight!
My cereal tries to hitch a ride,
A bowl of chaos in the tide!

The sun forgot to hold my hat,
It flew away, the cheeky brat!
I chase it down through stars and dust,
And ponder on what's fair and just.

My slippers moonwalk on the floor,
They twist and shout, and ask for more.
The ceiling fans all cheer and sing,
In this wild world of floating bling.

Celestial Cadence

The stars above began to waltz,
They tripped and fell, not my fault!
A comet laughed, a shooting star,
They spun around, I cheered from far!

The sun put on a silly hat,
While planets giggled, round and fat.
The asteroid belt plays hide and seek,
I join the fun, oh what a streak!

The Milky Way's a slippery slide,
With cosmic kids who laugh with pride.
They drink the stardust lemonade,
In zero-g, the games are made!

My glasses flew right off my nose,
The cosmos teased, "Where'd they go?"
I squint and laugh, the view's so bright,
In this grand dance of day and night.

Unmoored Verses

My pen is floating in the air,
It scribbles notes without a care.
The paper's gone, it's off to roam,
Those rhymes are unchained, far from home!

I tried to write a ballad sweet,
But ink's becoming quite the cheat.
It spills and tastes the fabric's flair,
As thoughts go racing everywhere!

The bookshelf joins a conga line,
With volumes swirling, it's divine!
A novel leaps, a footer flops,
While every page just wants to hop!

I chased my dreams through pages torn,
In this wild world, I am reborn.
The quirky twists of every thought,
Unmoored and wild, I've surely caught.

Skylight Serenades

The clouds are singing just for fun,
With fluffy voices, sweet as bun.
A raindrop slips, a note goes high,
While butterflies join in the sky!

The larks are doing aerial flips,
As sunbeams shine on sunny trips.
A dance of breezes, soft and light,
Each serenade brings pure delight!

The kite's a jester, pulling pranks,
It drifts and soars above the ranks.
A gust of wind makes flowers laugh,
While daisies cheer on the aerial staff!

The whole day hums a merry tune,
As stars pop up, like joy balloons.
With every breath, the skies conspire,
To lift our spirits ever higher!

Flights of Fable

In a land where oceans float,
Fish wear hats and swim a boat.
Clouds are pillows, soft and bright,
Stars play tag in the warm twilight.

Cats can fly on whimsy wings,
Chasing after goofy things.
Balloons hold secrets, tales to share,
As squirrels dance in mid-air flair.

Pine trees whisper, 'Come and play,'
While ants serve tea by the bay.
Laughter bounces, high and wide,
In this world of silly pride.

So bring your dreams and wear your grin,
For here the fun will never thin.
With every tale, we take a flight,
Into the laughter of the night.

Floating Lullabies

Bubbles dance on silver streams,
Whispering soft, enchanting dreams.
Twinkling puppies, oh what a sight,
Snoring stars cuddle up tight.

Ducks in slippers waddle and sing,
Telling tales of a jolly spring.
Butterflies wear polka-dots wide,
Floating high on joy's sweet ride.

Giggles echo in the breeze,
Tea parties held among the trees.
Silly shadows join the walk,
As marshmallows begin to talk.

So close your eyes and let it be,
A world where fun is wild and free.
In floating lullabies, we sway,
To the rhythm of a bright ballet.

Airy Similes

Like a kite in a playful chase,
Thoughts drift high in space, space, space!
Silly squirrels ride on the breeze,
Wiggly worms dive with unease.

As bright as a frog wearing a crown,
Jumping joyfully up and down.
Like jellybeans in a soft bag,
Bounce with colors, laugh and brag.

Smoother than a slide in the sun,
Where giggles echo, never done.
Like clouds that tickle a playful cheek,
Words take flight, as dreams peek.

So let your heart float high and proud,
Join the laughter of this crowd.
For in each simile's embrace,
We find the joy of silly grace.

Heavenly Harmonies

In the sky where giggles blend,
Clouds hum tunes that never end.
Breezes carry secrets shared,
As the sun softly declared.

Dancing daisies take a bow,
To the puzzled, prancing cow.
Harmony in a whimsical song,
As nature sings all day long.

Fruit flies waltz in birthday zest,
With honey bees that never rest.
Baking cakes from clouds of fluff,
Life is sweet, more than enough.

So join the chorus, sing along,
Celebrate with laughter strong.
In heavenly harmonies, we gleam,
Floating high within the dream.

Celestial Poetry

In a world where cats can fly,
Fish swim by in the bright blue sky.
Birds wear hats, and cows jump high,
While squirrels laugh as they pass by.

Umbrellas dance without a care,
Guided by the wind's wild flair.
A table spins, a chair takes flight,
In this odd realm, all feels just right.

Bubbles float with a silly grin,
As donuts roll and start to spin.
Chickens waltz, and frogs will croon,
In this bizarre, nutty afternoon.

Let's toast with juice, cheers to the air!
Where nothing's normal, all's quite rare.
With giggles echoing through the blue,
Join in the fun, there's room for you!

Beyond Downward Pull

Balloons are bouncing all around,
While turtles flip and dance on ground.
A sock with eyes begins to tease,
As jellybeans float with such ease.

Up in the sky, a cowbird sings,
Wearing a crown made of spring things.
Marshmallows leap from tree to tree,
In this wild world, we're all carefree.

Pizza slices glide through the rays,
As dancing spoons start their ballet.
Let's flip the script and twist a tune,
In our world of laughter, night till noon.

So grab your hat, let's take a flight,
Where every giggle feels so right.
No need for worries, just let it go,
In this fantastic, topsy flow!

The Altitude of Expression

Kites play tag with the fluffy clouds,
While llamas dance and cheer in crowds.
A pickle parachutes down quick,
With goofy grins, it's quite the trick.

Jellyfish twirl in a hula hoop,
As ants in hats jump through a loop.
The sun wears shades, sipping on tea,
While toast does a jig, wild and free.

What if the snowflakes wore bow ties?
Or if cows could trade their moos for sighs?
Dancing forks twirl and giggle with glee,
In laughter's embrace, we all just be.

So join the fun, let's not be shy,
In a silly world where dreams can fly.
With chuckles aplenty, let's take a stand,
In this quirky place, it's all so grand!

Swaying in the Atmosphere

Bananas slip on a rainbow slide,
As elephants wear polka-dot pride.
Cups of cocoa bounce on a spree,
While marbles stroll with gusto and glee.

Rockets leap like frogs on a quest,
Sailing through clouds where dreams manifest.
As rubber chickens join in the beat,
The whole world's dancing on jelly feet.

The moon's a disco ball, oh so bright,
Guiding the stars with twinkling light.
Lollipops play hopscotch in the breeze,
As giggles float and hearts feel at ease.

So let's embrace the whims of the air,
Where silliness sparkles, beyond compare.
With every twist, let joy take flight,
In this zany world, everything feels right!

Feathered Words

Words float like feathers, light as can be,
A turvy-topsy tumble, come dance with me!
They giggle and wiggle, with each little phrase,
In a world made of laughter, we'll spend our days.

A balloon of ideas, they soar through the air,
Spinning and twirling, with nary a care.
They tickle the funny bone, oh what a sight,
As letters bounce high, they dance in delight.

With each plucky pun, the giggles do rise,
Chasing the clouds, like spirited flies.
From droll little tales, our smiles take flight,
In a whirlwind of words, we'll find pure delight.

So gather your thoughts, let them float on by,
In a comical tempest, imagination is high!
With feathered words, let our joy break the rules,
As we leap through the air, like wonderfully fools!

Poetic Zephyrs

Whispers of nonsense are breezy and light,
Dancing with jests that soar out of sight.
They tumble like leaves on a carefree spree,
These zephyrs of laughter, come play with me!

They twirl past my window with giggles that tease,
Chasing me lightly, like a tickling breeze.
A quip here and there, like clouds made of cheese,
My heart floats along with the silliest ease.

From whimsy to wonder, they flutter and flop,
These poetic air-bombs, they just cannot stop!
As I catch one or two, and let out a cheer,
I'm swept into joy, leaving worries in fear.

So come take a ride on these verses of fun,
As we hop on the clouds, our laughter's begun!
With poetic zephyrs, our spirits are high,
In a jubilant whirlwind, we'll soar through the sky!

Lifting the Spirit

Up we go, on the wings of a joke,
Floating along like a jovial poke.
With each little giggle, the burdens all lift,
In this playful realm, we find our true gift.

A pun here, a chuckle, the smiles take flight,
We break through the clouds, oh what a delight!
With whimsical wonders that tickle the heart,
In this lifting of spirits, we play our small part.

Like bubbles of laughter, we rise ever high,
In a frolicsome frolic, we'll touch the sky.
As joy carries on with each wink and each quip,
Our souls take a journey, on this merry trip.

So come join the fiesta of fun and of glee,
On this wild, buoyant wave, just you and me!
With laughter as fuel, we'll ascend and take flight,
In this lifting of spirits, everything's bright!

Ascension in Stanzas

In stanzas of humor, we twirl and we sway,
Like balloons in a breeze, we're carried away.
Each line is a hop, each verse is a leap,
In this playful ascent, our laughter runs deep.

With wordplay that tickles, we float ever high,
Like kites in the sun, we dance through the sky.
From jokes that take off, our spirits set free,
In this ascension of stanzas, there's joy, can't you see?

A chorus of chuckles, we gather them round,
As we bound through the verses with glee, we're unbound.
With each rippling laugh, like a stream in the breeze,
We cling to the moments that bring us to ease.

So grab onto laughter, let's reach for the stars,
In this whimsical journey, our humor's on par!
With ascendancy pure in the rhythm of rhyme,
Let's sail through the verses, it's our joyful time!

Airborne Elegies

A squirrel danced on a tightrope high,
With acorns held tight, oh my, oh my!
He stumbled and jiggled, quite the sight,
As the crows above cheered with delight.

A cat in a hat tried to take wing,
With a jump and a flap, what chaos did bring!
He landed in feathers, much to his shame,
But laughed it off, such a comical game.

The ants with balloons planned a grand flight,
Their parade was a flurry, a joyful light!
They drifted skyward, on whims they'd ride,
Till a gust of wind turned their joy to slide.

A fish in a bowler joined the show,
With fins full of flair, he made quite the blow!
The clouds were his stage, the stars his glee,
In this wild waltz of whimsical spree.

The Freedom of Flight

The chickens all dreamed of soaring high,
With wings spread wide, touching the sky.
They flapped and flopped, what a hilarious race,
Only to end up, back in their space.

A dog with a jetpack zoomed past the fence,
He barked and he whizzed; it was quite intense.
The cats on the ground just stared in awe,
As the dog flipped around, with a final "Whoa!"

A snail with a cape joined the lofty quest,
He launched with a wiggle, attempting his best.
Through the grass blades, he slowly glided,
In a spiral of giggles, her friends all provided.

A parrot proclaimed, "Let's all take flight!"
With wind in their feathers, they danced through the night.

They whirled and they twirled, such a colorful crew,
And the stars winked back, joining in too.

Echoes in the High Sphere

In meadows of clouds, the frogs sang a tune,
With echoes that bounced like a big balloon.
They leapt from the daisies, soaring so free,
Falling back down with giggles of glee.

A goat on a trampoline bounced with delight,
He flipped through the air, what a whimsical sight!
His friends all below let out gasps and yells,
As he spun like a top, then rang all the bells.

The owls teamed up for a high-flying act,
With wings wide open, they made quite an impact.
They trained all year, oh what a display,
Till the last dove and turned, in their comical way.

A mouse in a helmet skated above,
With cheese-shaped balloons, he soared like a dove.
He waved to the crowd from way up so high,
And promised to bring them some snacks from the sky.

A Balancing Act

On a line made of dreams, a penguin did dance,
With flippers held high, he took quite the chance.
He twirled with a smile, and hiccupped with glee,
While seals applauded from the nearby sea.

A hedgehog on stilts tried to join in the fun,
He wobbled and giggled, oh what a run!
His balance was quirky, a sight quite absurd,
He rolled into twirls, like a fluffy little bird.

The poodles in pink were lining the way,
With ribbons and bows, they were here to play.
They balanced their treats, in a doggy parade,
With laughter and joy, a spectacular charade.

And as the sun set, they took one last spin,
With cheers and some snickers, they all gathered in.
They counted their blessings, a flight of pure fun,
In this circus of silliness, never was done.

Whispers of Celestial Heights

In the sky, a cow took flight,
Mooing softly, what a sight!
Chasing stars, she danced with glee,
Bouncing near the galaxy.

A cat on a cloud, what a surprise,
Winking down with playful eyes.
She twirled with the sun, bright and bold,
Purring tales of treasures untold.

Aliens waved from their shiny ships,
Sharing cheese with tiny nips.
A cosmic party in full swing,
While Earthlings gasped at everything.

So next time you see the moon fly high,
Don't be shocked; just wave goodbye.
For in the night, the fun won't end,
As planets play and stars descend.

A Dance Beyond the Pull

Bouncing off the walls of space,
An octopus wears a silly face.
With each tentacle, a twist and whirl,
He jived in circles, giving a twirl.

A cow in a tutu leaps and bounds,
Defying all earth's heavy sounds.
With rhythm so catchy, they danced so free,
Unfurling the giggles of you and me.

Mice on rockets, zooming past,
With cheese in hand, their dreams amassed.
They spun in laughter, a cosmic race,
Joking, "Who knew we'd be this place?"

So break the chains that pull you down,
Join the circus in the sky town!
For everyday's a carnival flight,
When silly dreams take off at night.

Soaring on Penumbra Wings

A penguin glides through warming skies,
Wings spread wide, what a surprise!
In a tuxedo, sleek and bright,
He's the star of this funny night.

Jellybeans float with squeaky chairs,
Caught in a dance with candy bears.
With every bounce, they laugh and cheer,
As peppermints twirl, nothing to fear.

A fish in a top hat swims through stars,
Sipping moon juice from silver jars.
With each puff of smoke, it regales,
Tales of adventures through dreamy trails.

So put on a smile, weave tales so grand,
Join the wacky, offbeat band!
For on these wings, we'll soar and sing,
With sugary dreams that joy will bring.

Lifting Dreams from Earthly Ties

A rabbit hopped on clouds of cream,
Chasing shadows, living the dream.
In a hot air balloon made of jam,
He bought a ticket, who gives a damn?

A squirrel spun tales with puffy cheeks,
Searching for treasures, or so it speaks.
In a plane of leaves, he flies so free,
While singing loud in perfect glee.

A giraffe in a collar, bright and bold,
Flapping around, a sight to behold.
With neck so long, he waves and sways,
Greeting monsters from fun-filled days.

So let's lift off, with laughter high,
Into the realm where dreams comply.
For in this world of whimsy and cheer,
We'll dance among the stars, my dear.

Ethereal Notations

In a world where socks float high,
And jelly beans dance on the sly,
A cat in a hat sings a tune,
While spoons are all flying by the moon.

Dancing noodles twist and twirl,
As spaghetti starts to spin and whirl,
Chasing after a giggling bee,
Who tells everyone, 'Come up and see!'

Puddles leap with a joyful splash,
As turtles in shades make a dash,
With every bounce, they bring such cheer,
In a world where laughter is near.

The sun wears a hat tipped way too low,
Tickling clouds in a breezy show,
And rainbows stretch like silly strings,
As stars above do their dance of flings.

Flutings in the Breeze

A penguin plays a flute on ice,
While squirrels jam in warm, thick spice,
They spin in circles, laughing loud,
Forming a most peculiar crowd.

Birds wear glasses, singing tunes,
Around the park, they dart like loons,
While chipmunks bust out funky moves,
Hopping around in groovy grooves.

Mice skate backward with such flair,
While twirling coons toss candy in the air,
Sipping lemonade from tiny cups,
As music flows and never stops.

Balloons are tied to dancing feet,
While candy floss drifts, oh so sweet,
In a whirlwind of laughs and glee,
Where silly is the new decree.

Caressing the Sky

Lemonade clouds float by so sweet,
While ants put on their tap shoes and beat,
They waltz and jitterbug, what a sight,
As bubbles drift off into the light.

A silly goose plays peekaboo,
While stars donate their sparkly goo,
Each twirl releases a radiant beam,
In the land of ticklish dream.

Upside-down trees grow candy leaves,
While giggling breezes make you believe,
That unicorns ride on bicycle chains,
Riding over hills of marshmallow plains.

Round and round, a merry-go-round,
While whispers of whimsy are found,
In a carnival sky, all in delight,
Where everything sparkles in the night.

Serenades Alight

Giraffes in bow ties croon to the sun,
While light bulbs play tag, just for fun,
Bubblegum blossoms pop with glee,
As jellyfish sway under the sea.

A snail in a tux takes center stage,
Reciting poetry, filled with gauge,
With lines so silly they make us giggle,
While frogs in fedoras hop and wiggle.

The moon, a DJ spinning all night,
Serves up stars that twinkle, oh so bright,
With a wink and a twist, they take their flight,
In a symphony of laughter and light.

Rain falls up, splashing on cars,
While cats give high-fives to passing stars,
And every sound that fills the air,
Is a funny serenade, rich and rare.

Songs Above the Clouds

Up high where the breezes play,
Birds sing songs, they glide away.
With silly hats and socks so bright,
They dance around, what a silly sight!

Clouds wear shoes made of fluffy fluff,
While rain drops giggle, oh, that's enough!
Every splash is a joyful sound,
In this world where laughter is found!

The sun loves to tickle the trees,
As butterflies float with the greatest of ease.
With starlit jokes and moonbeam teams,
They paint the air with funny dreams!

So let's lift off with a cheerful cheer,
Join the fun where there's nothing to fear.
In songs above the clouds we soar,
Finding giggles forevermore!

Whispers of the Lightness

In a world where toes don't touch the ground,
Laughter echoes, it's truly profound.
Balloons tell secrets as they float by,
"Watch out below, we might pass you by!"

A squirrel in shades rides a butterfly,
With a smile so wide, he's reaching the sky.
They whisper tales of noodles and cheese,
That tickle the air in the sweetest breeze!

Above the trees where the fairies play,
They skedaddle around in a whimsical way.
With donut wings and a chocolate grin,
In a land so light, the fun won't thin!

So come and hear the whispers of cheer,
As the clouds do flip-flops, and nothing's unclear.
In this silly place where giggles ignite,
Everything floats, what a joyful sight!

A Dance in the Celestial

Stars don their bows, twinkling so bright,
They gather for a dance in the moonlight.
With stardust shoes and beams of glee,
They wiggle and jiggle, oh can't you see?

Comets race in a zig-zag line,
While meteors criss-cross, oh what a sign!
In an orbit of giggles, they spin with grace,
Dancing through space, just keeping pace!

Planets burst out in a lively jig,
With Saturn's rings doing a funny gig.
Jupiter spins, with a whoop and a whirl,
As Mars throws confetti, it's quite the swirl!

So join the party, let your soul take flight,
In a dance of the celestial through the starry night.
Where silly moves create joy to behold,
And laughter dances—oh, how bold!

The Weightless Waltz

In a space where gravity took a break,
We glide and float, for fun's own sake.
With jellybeans bouncing on the moon,
Twinkling up there, like a bright maroon!

A penguin in slippers twirls round and round,
Swaying to music that can't be found.
With taffy clouds and a soda stream,
The weightless waltz is the sweetest dream!

Worms in top hats plan a parade,
As they shuffle along, spider webs cascade.
Light as a feather, they prance up high,
Jumping from feathers that tickle the sky!

So let's join hands for the final spin,
In this waltz of joy, where all can win.
Through the giggles and glee, our spirits enfold,
In a tale that's always delightfully bold!

A Symphony of Light

In a world where echoes leap,
Laughter dances on the breeze,
Balloons in a waltz, they sweep,
 Floating high with perfect ease.

Sunshine tickles every face,
As shadows tumble in delight,
Chasing giggles, they embrace,
 A symphony of purest light.

Butterflies in bow ties prance,
Playing tag with clouds so white,
 In this whimsical romance,
Everything feels just so right.

With a twist and spinning cheer,
 Bananas wear a bright top hat,
And every joke you hold so dear,
Makes even grumpy bears go splat!

Effervescent Tracks

Bubbles bounce on little feet,
Racing down a sliding hill,
This fizzy world can't be beat,
With every pop, time stands still.

Lemon drops in skies of blue,
Candy rain falls soft and sweet,
In this land where dreams come true,
Dancing to the sugar beat.

Hats that float above the crowd,
Twirling with a joyous sound,
Each step taken, bold and loud,
In this playful merry-go-round.

With twinkling stars above us gleam,
In bubble wraps and frothy streams,
Our laughter flares like a dream,
Chasing after silly themes!

Unhindered Voices

Whistling whispers pause for fun,
Lizards sing and cows wear caps,
Every creature joins the run,
In a world of silly laps.

Penguins tap their tiny toes,
Wobble-wobble, giggle spree,
Everywhere, bright laughter flows,
In a jesting jubilee.

Tickled by the breeze that sways,
Rocking chairs sing lullabies,
In our hearts, the song still plays,
As time hops and dance supplies.

Shirts adorned with polka dots,
Socks mismatched, a perfect sight,
In this land where fun never rots,
Unhindered voices share delight!

Rise of the Imagination

Kites that chase the morning sun,
Dancing high on candy streams,
Every dream is just begun,
Fluffy clouds hold secret schemes.

Elephants wear roller skates,
Pandas juggle with great flair,
Giraffes, oh, they open gates,
As fairies learn to fly through air.

Marshmallow mountains rise so fast,
In this land where wishes soar,
With every laugh, our hearts are cast,
In a giggle-filled folklore.

Chasing shadows, painting skies,
With colors bold and stories bright,
In this realm where wonder lies,
Imagination takes its flight!

Poetic Soarings: A Celestial Odyssey

Up in the sky, I tripped on a cloud,
My head in the stars, feeling so proud.
Dancing with comets, what a strange sight,
Sipping on stardust, all through the night.

Frolicking moons give me a wink,
On a feathered chair — watch me think!
Flip upside down, what a wild game,
Chasing the sun — is that really its name?

Wobbling softly, I giggle and sway,
Planets all chuckle in their own way.
I'm juggling meteors, oh what a show,
Floating on laughter, just let it flow.

Away from dull earth, it's all such a blast,
With whimsical wonders, I'll forever last.
Skip through the cosmos, grab a star treat,
Who knew space fun would feel so sweet?

A Symphony in the Upper Strata.

Twirling and swirling, in cosmic ballet,
The stars all applaud — hip hip hooray!
Celestial giggles echo through space,
As I attempt my moonwalk — what a disgrace!

Playing the harp made of shimmering light,
Each note a bubble drifting from sight.
Bouncing off planets, a giggle parade,
Making the cosmos a grand escapade.

A comet's quick swoosh, my dance partner's here,
Spinning like tops, oh what fun, my dear!
The Milky Way's laughter spills all around,
With starry confetti — joy knows no bound.

I tripped on a nebula — what a sticky mess,
Rubbed my stardust knees, can't help but confess.
This symphonic frolic, I hope it won't end,
With giggles and glimmers — my cosmic friends!

Floating Dreams

Drifting on whispers of soft cosmic breeze,
I'm swimming through starlight, with grace and ease.
Bubbles of laughter float by my side,
Riding on beams of the sun's golden tide.

Tumbling through twilight, a soft little blur,
Caught in a twirl, I'm a bright space explorer.
Doodling in stardust, my canvas is wide,
Creating a masterpiece that no one can hide.

Juggling moonbeams like floating balloons,
Each one a whisper of joyful tunes.
I trip on a wish, and it makes me grin,
What a delight; where to even begin?

Chasing my shadows, they giggle and flee,
In this cosmic circus, I dance with glee.
Dreams are the flights that we take with our hearts,
In a universe painted with whimsical arts!

Edges of the Ether

Hopping on photons, skipping light years,
Each bounce and twirl, I'm quelling my fears.
Caught in a whirlpool of dreamy delight,
Laughing with meteors, what a silly sight!

In the eddies of ether, I found a nice pair,
Of floating pink slippers that match my hair.
Stardust confetti falling all about,
Makes the dance floor of space just scream and shout!

Frogs in bows ties sing no gravity checks,
Tossing their hats at peculiar insects.
As we twirl through the void, what fun it transforms,
A cosmic gala, where oddity warms.

With rocket-fueled ice cream, I'm ready to soar,
Explosive flavors as I shout "More!"
Edges of dreams, in this fun-loving space,
Laughing till my heart races and finds its own pace!

Dreamscapes Unfettered

In dreams my cat can fly,
She zooms past clouds, oh my!
With a cape made of cheese,
She conquers the blue breeze.

Flying fish do a parade,
Wearing hats, quite well displayed.
They giggle and swirl in glee,
As they sip on lemonade.

A tree serves cake, so sweet,
With squirrels dancing on their feet.
They juggle acorns, what a show,
As they steal the icing, oh no!

My bedroom turns to a ball,
Where teddies party, have a ball.
They spin on chairs made of pie,
As I laugh and munch on fries.

Ethereal Expressions

A balloon giraffe on the run,
Thought he'd stretch out to the sun.
Wobbly legs, what a sight,
He bounced and twirled with delight.

The moon wore a tutu tonight,
Glimmering stars joined in the flight.
They danced in a waltz with the breeze,
Swaying high above the trees.

Cupcakes fell from the blue sky,
Sprinkled rainbows, oh my, oh my!
We caught them on plates, how divine,
With frosting that sparkled like wine.

An orchestra of frogs begins,
Playing tunes that make us spin.
With banjos and flutes they sing,
While the daisies start to swing.

Soaring Signatures

A penguin glides on a slide,
With a cheeky grin, he takes pride.
Down he goes, what a splash,
Then spins around in a flash.

Kites that carry talking pillows,
Bouncing joy on bright armadillos.
They share jokes high above ground,
While swirling giggles all around.

Balloons with legs take a stroll,
Chasing after a rolling bowl.
With laughter that fills the day,
They dance their silly ballet.

A popcorn cloud floats so high,
Crunching beneath the big sky.
It rains butter, oh what fun,
As we munch till day is done.

Beyond the Reach

A frog in a top hat hops far,
Dreaming of riding a shooting star.
With wings made of candy and fluff,
He giggles, saying, 'This is enough!'

Little elves play hopscotch in air,
Floating high without any care.
With rainbows painted on their shoes,
They chase jellybeans, no time to snooze.

A snail dressed up for a race,
Wearing goggles, what a face!
He zips past, slow but steady,
With friends cheering, 'Are you ready?'

A cupcake flies on a broomstick,
Spinning around, and oh, so slick!
Sprinkles rain from above, so bright,
As we savor this wondrous sight.

Loops in the Sky

Up in the air, a kite does dance,
It took a chance, it learned to prance.
With a gust of wind, it spirals 'round,
Turns wobbly loops, without a sound.

Birds in bow ties, how do they fly?
With snazzy moves and a winked eye.
They soar and dive, in silly spree,
As clouds look on, oh what glee!

Balloons like jellybeans, float in grace,
Popping the ground, they change their place.
With giggles they gig, what a riot,
Chasing a breeze, oh so quiet!

A trampoline world, where laughter springs,
Bouncing along, on silly things.
Jumping and flipping, like a clown,
Who needs the floor when you wear a crown?

Defying the Ground

A cat on a roof, what a curious sight,
Waving its tail, saying, 'Goodnight!'
With a leap to the stars, it plots its course,
Chasing a dream, like a playful horse.

Grasshoppers in top hats, hopping so high,
Tiptoeing gently, through the blue sky.
With each little jump, they giggle with glee,
Defying all rules, as happy as can be.

The moon plays peek-a-boo, with a cheeky grin,
A hop, a skip, let the adventure begin.
Stars dance around, with a silly routine,
Making the night feel like a happy scene.

A rainbow on stilts, prancing with flair,
Wobbling proudly, without any care.
With colors that burst, in giggles they sound,
Who needs the ground, when fun is unbound?

Lyrical Levitation

A marshmallow cloud, oh what a thrill,
Floating so sweet, up high on the hill.
With rhymes that loop, like a rubber band,
It dances and twirls, so perfectly planned.

Socks on a line, waving with glee,
Hooting and tooting, as wild as can be.
With every fresh breeze, they jump in delight,
Making a fuss, well into the night.

Fluffy pancakes, rise up with cheer,
Flipping and flapping, they disappear.
With syrupy laughter, they float on by,
Who would have thought they'd learn to fly?

Silly old owls with monocles bright,
Perched on a branch, giving advice light.
With wisdom so quirky, they kind of sway,
As they laugh with the breeze, come what may.

Ascending Verses

An octopus juggling, who would have guessed?
With tentacles waving, it sure is impressed.
It bounces on waves, with a wink and spin,
Creating a chaos, where fun can begin.

Kitesurfers giggle, as they ride the wave,
Gliding through air, feeling quite brave.
With flips and spins, they craft their song,
Defying the ground, where they belong.

Jellybeans bouncing, on a trampoline spree,
Singing out loud, just wait and see.
Launching on laughter, the fun never ends,
Reaching for joy, with all of their friends.

A penguin on skis, what a bizarre feat!
Sliding on ice, with laughter so sweet.
It takes a bold leap, into the unknown,
Landing with flair, proud as a throne.

A Journey Beyond Gravity's Grasp

I hopped upon a bubble, oh so round,
With every bounce I lost my feet to ground.
I soared like toast, afloat in the blue,
Chasing after giggles, just me and my shoe.

The cat's on a comet, wearing a hat,
While dogs do somersaults, how 'bout that?
The sun winks at us, oh what a sight,
As we dance with clouds, drifting in flight.

An octopus juggles glittery stars,
While squirrels on rockets zoom past Mars.
Every flip and tumble, a new game to play,
Who knew that fun would take us away?

So here we float, in a whimsical plight,
Chasing dreams that twinkle through day and night.
With laughter like bubbles rising up high,
We leap through the air, and that's how we fly!

The Lift of Echoing Melodies

A tune rolled by like a sailing kite,
It tickled my toes and sparked pure delight.
The notes started dancing, a jig and a sway,
And who knew that music could lead us astray?

The saxophone winked with a mischievous flair,
While violins twirled, like they just don't care.
Piano keys flipped, somersaults in tune,
As trumpets turned upside down, oh what a boon!

We twirled with the rhythms, hands up to the sky,
Bouncing on beats, like popcorn to fly.
Laughing so hard that we almost fell,
In this melody madness, we danced so well!

With every high note and dip in the sound,
We frolicked through echoes, joy unbound.
So let the music lift us, oh what a ride,
As we float through the air with friends by our side!

Whirling in the Weightless Wind

I spun with the breezes, a dizzying whirl,
A feather in flight, a giggling twirl.
The trees started dancing, waltzing with glee,
As I joined the parade, just a sprightly me!

The daisies declared, "Let's all hop and leap!"
While butterflies giggled, their secrets to keep.
With each little whoosh, the world took a spin,
Playing tag with the sunlight, let the fun begin!

A tumbleweed chuckled, rolling on through,
As I tumbled and laughed, me and the dew.
We soared past the hills, a whimsical race,
In this rambunctious spin, all worries we chase.

With smiles like balloons, we floated along,
In this merry go round of a silly song.
Let's waltz with the whispers and giggles that sing,
In the weightless wind, come join the winged fling!

Poetry Above the Planet's Pull

Words fluttered upward, like birds on a spree,
Shouting silly secrets, just for you and me.
Ink dribbled like honey, sweet and divine,
As we scribbled our dreams on a breeze of fine wine.

Letters danced freely, no tether or chain,
Like squirrels in socks, they played in the rain.
Each stanza a splash in the puddles of rhyme,
A frolicsome festival, hand in hand with time.

With giggles and wiggles, the verses take flight,
Painting the air, oh what a delight!
In this wonderful realm where the wild words play,
We'll pen our adventures the zany way!

So let's soar through the verses, carefree and free,
Defying all pulls, just you and me.
In the land of the whimsical, we'll always recall,
That laughter and poetry can conquer it all!

Beyond the Horizon of Ordinary Thought

I tried to float in a rubber boat,
But I ended up wearing a funny coat.
The sea was calm, the sky so bright,
Until a seagull swooped and gave me a fright.

I danced with clouds, skipped on a breeze,
Tickled the sun, said, "Stay, if you please!"
But it rolled its eyes and laughed with glee,
"You can't catch me, I'm too free!"

An elephant jumped over a moonlit fence,
Strutting around, as if it made sense.
A slapstick scene, all in good fun,
We twirled together until the day was done.

So if your thoughts ever start to weigh,
Just hop on a cloud, come out and play!
For in a world where whimsy reigns,
The ordinary mind never quite gains.

Rhymes that Brush Against the Stars

A comet chased a squirrel in fright,
While Venus winked, oh, what a sight!
They played tag around the moon's bright glow,
As Martians chuckled, putting on a show.

I wrote a poem in a zero-gravity chair,
With words that floated around in the air.
Each rhyme took flight, danced like a bird,
Making my cat think I'd lost my words.

The sun wore shades, looking rather cool,
While Saturn's rings spun like a twirling jewel.
I asked the stars to teach me to rhyme,
They replied, "Just laugh, and you'll be just fine!"

So if you find your muse is quite shy,
Call on the cosmos; let your laughter fly!
For in charming verses, silly and bold,
You'll find the wonders that can't be told.

The Uplift of Untethered Souls

A kite decided it wanted to sing,
So it wrapped itself around my spring.
With a twist and a shout and a gusty breeze,
We flew up high, oh what a tease!

The earthworms cheered with a wiggle and squirm,
As we danced in the air, breaking every term.
A balloon brigade joined our festive crew,
Making music with colors, pink, red, and blue.

An octopus juggled as it floated by,
Juggling stars while I tried not to cry.
"Why so serious?" the stars sang in glee,
Just let your heart fly; it's as fun as can be!

So if you're feeling heavy, just lift your gaze,
Dream of floaty things, and join the praise.
For in the realm of the silly and bright,
Untethered souls find their ultimate flight!

Ballads in the Stratosphere

A frog on a pogo stick jumped to the sky,
With a top hat and tails, looking quite spry.
He croaked out a ballad, full of delight,
While clouds underneath danced in pure white light.

The breeze joined the tune with a whimsical twist,
As paper airplanes flew, they couldn't resist.
They dove and dipped, doing loops and turns,
While the sun applauded with its golden burns.

An acrobat starfish flung glitter and glow,
As rainbows joined hands in the bright afterglow.
Together they sang of their offbeat ways,
Like children at play on the longest of days.

So if you catch a whimsy or a laugh in the air,
Just ride with the moments; let go of your care.
For in this grand ballad, both joyous and true,
You'll find magic above in the vast sky of blue!

Unbound Stanzas

Up in the sky, my socks took flight,
Chasing a cloud, a comical sight.
They twirled and whirled like playful sprites,
Far from my feet, what a funny plight!

A cat with a jetpack zooms out of view,
Wearing a cape, it thinks it's a hero too.
It leaps through the air, like it's nothing new,
Who knew cats could fly? It's quite the debut!

Penguins in space, donning tiny hats,
Riding on rockets, oh, imagine that!
Dancing on Saturn, with mischievous pats,
They're the coolest crew, if I may say that!

A cheese wheel rolls with a giggly cheer,
Floating through orbit, without any fear.
It spins and it glides, oh dear, oh dear!
Who knew snacks could fly? Let's all give a cheer!

Poised on Air

Jellybeans bounce on invisible waves,
Jumping and laughing, so merry, so brave.
In rainbows they find their sweet little caves,
These cuddly candies, so joyous, they crave!

A fish in a tutu dances on high,
Balancing dreams beneath a pink sky.
With every pirouette, the world gives a sigh,
Oh what a sight, as it glides by!

Giraffes on trampolines, oh what a show,
Each bounce brings laughter, as we all know.
They stretch for the stars with a glittery glow,
Defying the limits, let the fun flow!

A snail in a rocket, who's off to the moon,
Leaving behind, a sweet looping tune.
With friends in the cosmos, they'll be there by noon,
Together they giggle, a whimsical boon!

Defiant Lines

The ants are all dancing on top of parade,
With acrobatic stunts, a grand escapade.
In tiny top hats, they're all unafraid,
What a spectacle! Don't be dismayed!

A toaster took off with a loaf of bread,
Flying around 'til it's gleefully fed.
With pop-tarts on board, they're covering dread,
A breakfast adventure, that's how it's led!

Squirrels in sunglasses are gripping balloons,
Soaring through skies, while they whistle sweet tunes.
In search of the acorns, they giggle like goons,
Who knew they could fly? Oh, what a boon!

An elephant bounces with joy on a kite,
Twirling through air, what a charming sight.
With laughter and trumpets, they soar with delight,
What a defiant dance in the sheer daylight!

Weightless Words

A sandwich with wings takes off and then flies,
Spreading good cheer, oh, how it complies!
With lettuce and laughter, it reaches the skies,
Who knew lunch could soar? What a great surprise!

A puppy on clouds is chasing his tail,
Bounding and barking, a soft, furry trail.
Frolicking freely, with dandelions to sail,
He giggles in glory, there's no chance to fail!

Dancing to rhythms, the stars hold their breath,
As jump ropes skip lightly, defying their death.
A chorus of giggles sings sweet with each step,
Who knew that the sky could be playful and deft?

A rhyming balloon sails caught in a breeze,
Popping with laughter while tickling trees.
Who knew that words could float with such ease?
In the land of nonsense, they dance and they tease!

www.ingramcontent.com/pod-product-compliance
Lightning Source LLC
Chambersburg PA
CBHW051655160426
43209CB00004B/902